STUDENT LEADERSHIP UNIVERSITY
STUDY GUIDE SERIES

LEADERSHIP ROCKS

JAY STRACK

THOMAS N
Since 1

NASHVILLE   DALLAS   MEXICO CITY   RIO DE JANEIRO

Published in Nashville, Tennessee, by Thomas Nelson. Thomas Nelson is a trademark of Thomas Nelson, Inc.

Thomas Nelson, Inc. books may be purchased in bulk for educational, business, fund-raising, or sales promotional use. For information, please e-mail SpecialMarkets@ThomasNelson.com.

All Scripture quotations are taken from *The New King James Version®*. Copyright © 1982 by Thomas Nelson, Inc. Used by permission. All rights reserved.

ISBN: 978-1-4185-0593-6

Printed in the United States of America

13 14 15 QG 9 8 7 6 5 4 3 2 1

Page design by Crosslin Creative
2743 Douglas Lane, Thompsons Station, Tennessee 37179

CONTENTS

INTRODUCTION 5

KEY 6

1. **LEADER:**
  The Total Package 9

2. **FUELED:**
  Live with Intention 25

3. **EXECUTION:**
  The Art of Getting Things Done 41

4. **VISION:**
  A 360° View 55

5. **OPTIMISM:**
  A Countercultural Mind-Set 69

6. **RESPONSIBILITY:**
  The Ability to Respond 85

7. **CONSISTENCY:**
  The Right to Influence 99

8. **TENACITY:**
  Unstoppable Force 113

NOTES 126

ABOUT THE AUTHOR 129

INTRODUCTION

Believe it or not, you will influence thousands of people in your lifetime. In fact, you already do every single day! But do you feel like you don't really know how to be a leader? If so, you've come to the right place.

Leadership Rocks is designed to help you become a godly student with influence. In this study guide, you'll discover the principles of living confidently for God and learn to speak the language of a leader in bite-sized, easy-to-digest pieces. You'll learn that:

✦ A leader's first thought should be positive and courageous.

✦ A leader looks to the future.

✦ A leader is willing to do what others are not willing to do.

✦ Courage is a hallmark of leadership.

✦ Leaders are not controlled by fear.

✦ A true leader depends on Christ for the strength to do the right thing in any situation.

Although you may not realize it now, God has placed you in positions of leadership in your life for a reason. Don't be afraid of this role—dive into it! Dream big and open your heart to the amazing work God longs to do in you and through you.

Consider these words inscribed on the tomb of an Anglican bishop in Westminster Abbey Cathedral in London:

When I was young and free and my imagination had no limits, I dreamed of changing the world. As I grew older and wiser, I discovered the world would not change, so I shortened my sights somewhat and decided to change only my country. But, it too seemed immovable. As I grew into my twilight years, in one last desperate attempt, I settled for changing only family, those closest to me, but alas, they would have none of it. And now as I lie on my deathbed, I suddenly realize, if I had only changed myself first, then by example I would have changed my family. From their inspiration and encouragement I would then have been able to better my country and, who knows, I may have even changed the world.

KEY

STUDENT LEADERSHIP UNIVERSITY CURRICULUM

Throughout this study guide, you will see several icons or headings that represent an idea, a statement, or a question that we want you to consider as you experience Scripture in this study guide series. Refer to the descriptions below to help you remember what the icons and headings mean.

transfuse (trans FYOOZ): to cause to pass from one to another; transmit

The goal of the lesson for the week.

Experience Scripture: Learning to really experience Scripture is the key element to "getting" who God is and all that He has in store for you.

infuse (in FYOOZ): to cause to be permeated with something (as a principle or quality) that alters usually for the better

Through journaling, group discussion, and personal study, experience Scripture as it permeates your heart and alters your life.

Future Tense Living: Your choices today will determine your future. Learn how to live with dynamic purpose and influence.

Attitude Reloaded: Rethink your attitude! Learn to replace self-centered, negative, or limited thoughts with positive, courageous, compassionate thoughts that are based on God's unlimited ability and power.

 In His Steps: Every attitude and action of your life should begin with the questions, How would Jesus respond to this person and situation before me? What would He choose to do?

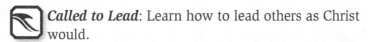
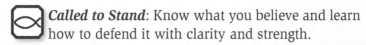

diffuse (di FYOOZ) : to pour out and permit or cause to spread freely; to extend, scatter

Once God's Word is infused into your heart, it will pour forth to others without restraint. In this section, explore what that looks like in your daily life.

Called to Lead: Learn how to lead others as Christ would.

Called to Stand: Know what you believe and learn how to defend it with clarity and strength.

Called to Share: Sharing truth and serving others are results of a transformed life. How can you share with others the awesome things you're learning?

One Thing: Consider ONE THING you can do this week to make a difference in your life and/or the life of another.

FUSE BOX

Power up for the week with this focused truth.

CHAPTER 1

LEADER
THE TOTAL PACKAGE

KEY SCRIPTURE

So he shepherded [led] them according to the integrity of his heart, and guided them by the skillfulness of his hands.
—Psalm 78:72

COULD THIS BE YOU?

I remember vividly the night I made a deal with God: "If you get me out of this detention center, I'll go to a Bible study." I also remember the first time I heard the good news from a man who said, "God loves you just like you are, but He loves you too much to leave you that way."

For most of my life, my heart had been dark with pain and hurt; but when I heard the good news of God's grace, a floodlight suddenly came into my soul. I prayed, "God, if you are real, come into my life and change me." I went home, flushed my drugs down the toilet, picked up a Bible, and began to live a new life.

I had been a powerless and out-of-control teen, but that day, the power of Christ transformed me. When I reached out to God, He gave me...

+ power of salvation for a changed heart and eternal life,

+ power to stand against temptation,

+ power to keep going when discouragement tried to take over,

+ power to accept responsibility and correct mistakes, and

✦ power to forgive the abusers in my life who had hurt me so deeply.

And He didn't leave me there. As a student making Ds and Fs in high school, I couldn't find a college that would take me. I was discouraged, but God was faithful to carry me through. Charleston Southern University took a chance on me, and I graduated cum laude in just two years. I went on to receive a master's degree and to earn a doctorate.

> Knowing God's Word in depth and understanding the background of the great promises of the Bible enables us to gain insight for living successfully today.

Later, when I married and then became a father, God taught me how to love more deeply than I ever imagined possible. He gave me a second chance and called me to preach the good news to others. He has been faithful to stand by me every moment as I have had the privilege of speaking to more than fifteen million people face to face and many more through television and radio.

Ever since I asked God to come into my life, He has been with me in whatever area I needed it. He has given me not only power over the past but power in the present. And every day, He continues to give me power for opportunities in the future.

I tell everyone the powerful truth that I have personally experienced: "If God is for us, who can be against us?" (Romans 8:31).

WHY KNOW IT?

✦ 51 percent of church members feel that the leadership in their congregation makes them enthusiastic about the future.[1]

✦ 74 percent of high school students have no interest in running for a national or local government office in the future.[2]

transfuse (trans FYOOZ) : to cause to pass from one to another; transmit

If you watch a cable news channel today, you will likely see reports about casualties in the Middle East, a terrorist act or two, violent crime in the U.S., storms battering some part of the planet, famine across the world, AIDS epidemics, and so on. Bombarded daily with this negative information, how does a young leader keep his or her thoughts positive? How do we prevent emotion from being the lead dog in our minds? How do we stay strong to the finish?

> It has been said that a person can live forty days without food, three days without water, and eight minutes without air—but not one minute without hope.

Fortunately, the Scriptures show us a plan to help us process bad days and to go through life with joy. The framework given to the nation of Israel in exile is the same timeless, powerful framework for a young leader today.

"For I know the thoughts that I think toward you," says the LORD, "thoughts of peace and not of evil, to give you a future and a hope." —**Jeremiah 29:11**

Jeremiah 29:11 is a popular Bible verse that has made it to the prime time—it can be found on posters, plaques, T-shirts, bumper stickers, and more. But many people do not know the context of this often-quoted promise.

In this verse, God declared His faithfulness to the people of Israel as their captors paraded them around in shackles through the ruins of a ransacked Jerusalem.

God's chosen people had been reduced to stumbling, shamed, and defeated captives. Imagine being conquered by your enemies and then forced to walk past the smoldering rubble that once was your home. The walls that once protected your hometown of Jerusalem are now broken down and burning; and even the temple, the holy place of worship, is in flames.

Happiness comes from the root word hap, meaning happenings, luck, or circumstance.

In the midst of this destruction, God reassured the Israelites of His faithfulness and backed up His words with action. His promise to you today is no less faithful than the one that brought great comfort and hope to the Hebrews during this time. Their journey to captivity in Babylon seemed like a dead end, but God brought them through and eventually enabled them to return to their homeland.

infuse (in FYOOZ) ; to cause to be permeated with something (as a principle or quality) that alters usually for the better

The Hebrews learned through violence what we can know in peace. Through our study of Scripture, we can understand that the Creator has given us all that we require to process the many different events and emotions that we experience, whether in the high tide or low tide of life. In our time of need, God's words to us are always tender, timeless, and teaching.

How does a leader experience the daily stresses of life, yet walk confidently into the future? This is possible when we *focus on the facts* that God gives us in His Word. It is imperative to have ownership of these facts before you can move forward into a life of leadership and successful living as a Christian.

FOCUS ON THE FACTS

"For I know the thoughts that I think toward you," says *the* LORD ...

Fact 1: The God of the Bible is on your side.

Fact 2: He is compassionately concerned about you.

Fact 3: You are on His mind and heart.

...thoughts of peace and not of evil...

Fact 4: He thinks good thoughts, *great* thoughts, even *amazing* thoughts about you.

Fact 5: His plans are peaceful and for your good.

...to give you a future and a hope...

Fact 6: He has a unique future planned for you.

Fact 7: God's plan for your future is a sure thing, an expected end.

CONTRAST

Evil in the Hebrew: worthless, noxious, hurtful, sad, sorrowful, wicked, depraved.

Peace in the Hebrew: to be whole, sound, safe; to be completed, finished; to be at peace; to be in friendship with; to be made secure; prosperity.

Get this: What God thinks of you IS NOT dependent upon your actions or on your thoughts of Him!

GROUP DISCUSSION

Do most people you know believe that God's love and care is dependent on their actions?

Ask yourself: Is my life ruled by facts or feelings? Out of the seven facts listed above, which am I unsure of? Why? Am I unsure of these because of what I've done or what I've thought or because of who God is?

Joy is a by-
product of believing
in the facts.

God has a *promised outcome* for you. This fact enables you to stay positive in a negative world. God is on your side!

This "hope" He speaks of in Jeremiah 29:11 is defined in the Hebrew as an expected end. It's not as if God is saying, "I hope so..." Instead, His plan for your future is a sure thing. There's no better warranty in the world than God's promise!

A leader focuses on the fact that hope has been secured by the Lord on his or her behalf. It's already yours, so go ahead and start to use it.

How do we live as Jesus lived: focused on the supernatural instead of bound by the ordinary? Once we focus on the facts in our mind, we then have to strengthen our spirit.

Staying motivated is without question a great challenge. We know that the apostle Paul was one of the most highly motivated individuals who ever walked the earth. How did he stay so enthusiastic? He constantly fed his faith, and he gives us the steps to do the same.

FEED YOUR FAITH

[This was] according to the eternal purpose which He accomplished in Christ Jesus our Lord, in whom we have boldness and access with confidence through faith in Him.... For this reason I bow my knees to the Father of our Lord Jesus Christ, from whom the whole family in heaven and earth is named, that He would grant you, according to the riches of His glory, to be strengthened with might through His Spirit in the inner man, that Christ may dwell in your hearts through faith; that you, being rooted and grounded in love, may be able to comprehend with all the saints what is the width and length and depth and height—to know the love of Christ which passes knowledge; that you may be filled with all the fullness of God. Now to Him who is able to do exceedingly abundantly above all that we ask or think, according to the power that works in us, to Him be glory in the church by Christ Jesus to all generations, forever and ever. Amen. —**Ephesians 3:11–12, 14–21**

Let's break this passage down:

...according to the eternal purpose...

✦ Live by eternal purpose, not the temporary.

... in whom we have boldness and access with confidence through faith in Him.

✦ Substitute self-confidence for God-confidence.

For this reason I bow my knees to the Father of our Lord Jesus Christ ...

✦ This simple act of humility before God will give birth to inner strength and dedication to God's will.

... that He would grant you, according to the riches of His glory, to be strengthened with might through His Spirit in the inner man ...

✦ Strengthen the inner man through your devotional times.

...that Christ may dwell in your hearts through faith...

✦ Live by faith and not by reason.

...being rooted and grounded in love ...

✦ Check your motives and your foundation often. Both should be love as Christ loved.

Now to Him who is able to do exceedingly abundantly above all that we ask or think according to the power that works in us ...

✦ Focus on the power of Christ and its availability to you. Think about it often, and thank Him for it. His power will be there when you need it.

Select ONE THING from the previous list to focus on this week. Which will it be? Write your answer in the space below.

---

diffuse (di FYOOZ) : to pour out and permit or cause to spread freely; to extend, scatter

Have you ever felt that maybe you've asked too much of a person? This is not possible with God—He has more to give than you are able to receive. He wants you to have a successful life more than you want to have one. He wants to give you more than you can envision. When you *focus on the facts* and *feed your faith*, you are well on your way to being able to *fight your fears*.

FIGHT YOUR FEARS

For God has not given us a spirit of fear, but of power and of love and of a sound mind. **—2 Timothy 1:7**

You think you've got problems? Paul made this great declaration during his second imprisonment in Rome, after his friends and supporters had deserted him, and as he waited for death. His physical circumstances, as bad as they were, could not diminish the truth of this verse then, and they cannot diminish it for us now.

God has not given us a spirit of fear...

Courage is a hallmark of leadership; you cannot lead others without it. Fear is a liar because it exaggerates the forces that surround us, and it is not of God. As someone has said, FEAR is **F**alse **E**vidence **A**ppearing **R**eal.

X-change Fear for Power
...but of power...

"Power" in this verse refers to divine capability. You can exchange fear for power, not because of your own capability, but because God is not limited in His divine power. Because of Christ, you have the power to do whatever needs to be done at the moment it needs doing.

X-change Fear for Love
...and of love...

Love is the ability and desire to forgive those who have betrayed, deserted, or hurt you. Paul spoke of love as he sat in a cold, dark, damp prison—really, just an underground cavern. He had been beaten, bound in shackles, deserted by his friends, and hated by his foes. "Even in this place," Paul was saying, "through Christ, I have the ability to love without regard to being loved back."

X-change Fear for a Sound Mind
...and of a sound mind.

The power to banish fear gave Paul the ability to have peace and a quiet mind in some of the loneliest days of his life. In the midst of the darkness, Paul was comforted by a courageously clean conscience. In this verse, he speaks of a *united mind*—a mind not fractured by fear.

God has given you a spirit of power, love, and a sound mind. No matter the need, God has already provided for you. Lead on!

Do I focus on the facts or live by my feelings?

Do I live expecting God to work in my future?

> Nothing so conclusively proves a man's ability to lead others as what he does from day to day to lead himself.
> —Thomas J. Watson Sr.

In an increasingly violent world, can I confidently present the power of Christ as exceedingly, abundantly, and above?

Will I take the time and effort to share with others the good news of the gospel—that Christ offers courage, love, and peace?

God's part: He is on your side and is willing to give you an amazing future.

Your part: Believe that God is not only willing but absolutely able to transform your life and ensure your future.

PRIVATE WORLD DEVOTIONS

MONDAY: See it. Read the surrounding passages or chapter for the Key Scripture so that you can get an understanding of the background and context. This helps you to really *see* the verse.

TUESDAY: Hear it. Read the daily Key Scripture and/or surrounding passage out loud, putting your name in, if applicable. For example, <u>John</u> *can do all things through Christ. Thieves have come to destroy* <u>John</u>, *but Jesus has come that* <u>John</u> *might have eternal life.*

WEDNESDAY: Write it. Write the verse and then what it says about:

✦ *Others:* Respond, serve, and love as Jesus would.

✦ *Me:* Specific attitudes, choices, or habits.

✦ *God:* His love, mercy, holiness, peace, joy, etc.

PRIVATE WORLD JOURNAL

I am grateful for—I praise you for—I am feeling—I am thinking—I need help with

PRIVATE WORLD DEVOTIONS *(Continued)*

THURSDAY: Memorize it. Take the verse with you—write it on a card or put it in your phone, iPod, or PDA. Go over it throughout the day so that it begins to *live* in your heart and mind.

FRIDAY: Pray it. Personalize the verse as you pray for yourself or for others or in praise to God. To pray is literally "to think about." Try thinking out loud or writing in your **PRIVATE WORLD JOURNAL.**

SATURDAY: Share it. Ask the Lord to bring someone to mind or in your path today who needs good news. Don't be shy—just let it out! Whether you IM, write, text, tell, or send it, the joy of God's Word will flow from your heart into theirs.

PRAYER REQUESTS

Date	Name	Need	Answer

PRIVATE WORLD JOURNAL

I am grateful for—I praise you for—I am feeling—I am thinking—I need help with

NOTES

CHAPTER 2

FUELED
LIVE WITH INTENTION

KEY SCRIPTURE

But without faith it is impossible to please Him,
for he who comes to God must believe that
He is, and that He is a rewarder of
those who diligently seek Him.

—Hebrews 11:6

COULD THIS BE YOU?

Check any of the following thoughts or behaviors that are, or have been, true of you:

- ❏ I have a test today, and I forgot to study.
- ❏ I had a fight with my best friend.
- ❏ I came home late; now I'm on restriction.
- ❏ That guy/girl keeps asking me out—should I go?
- ❏ Do I look OK? I wish I was more _____.
- ❏ There's a big party this weekend, and I wasn't invited.
- ❏ That porn site looked interesting…
- ❏ I need money to buy _____.
- ❏ My grades are borderline. I just can't get it.
- ❏ I'm the only one without a/an _____.
- ❏ There's not enough time.
- ❏ She talked about me behind my back. Now I feel so _____ _____.

WHY KNOW IT?

✦ Only 18 percent of teens talk to someone (a friend, parent, teacher, or guardian) about their anger.[1]

✦ 52 percent of adolescent males believe there are times when it's appropriate to express anger physically.[2]

✦ Stress accounts for two-thirds of family doctor visits.[3]

transfuse (trans FYOOZ): to cause to pass from one to another; transmit

Do you ever feel like you're walking through the state fair when you go to school? Barkers line every aisle, calling out to you to play a game, buy a ticket, and take a ride. They use insults, compliments, prizes, or taunts, and the voices come from every angle. It can be exhausting just to walk through!

Sometimes it becomes difficult, if not impossible, to process the number of emotions you experience within twenty-four hours. Life can feel unbalanced or out of control. We call this stress. Both good and bad stresses wear down the body and mind and are cumulative in nature—in other words, they pile up on you.

Sculptors call a *sincere* work of art one that is *without wax.* That means that mistakes were not glossed over with wax, that cracks in the marble or wood were not patched. The artwork is genuine all the way through, even though no one knows for sure but the artist.

When you experience stress, you might find yourself asking, "What is life about? Is God really in control?" These are common questions, but a person who lives intentionally is able to overcome daily stresses and live with confidence and influence.

CONTRAST

| *Good stress:* getting a job, doing well in school, new friends, holidays, etc. | *Bad stress:* learning difficulties, financial problems, family conflict, death of a loved one, illness, etc. |

The burden which the prophet Habakkuk saw. O LORD, how long shall I cry, and You will not hear? Even cry out to You, "Violence!" and You will not save.... Therefore the law is powerless, and justice never goes forth. For the wicked surround the righteous; therefore perverse judgment proceeds. —**Habakkuk 1:1–2, 4**

At the time the book of Habakkuk was written, the Babylonian empire was gaining tremendous strength, and it became apparent that the Hebrews were the next conquest on Nebuchadnezzar's list. Habakkuk was upset that a heathen man who mocked the one true God could become so powerful while God's people were in danger. In emotional exhaustion (stress), Habakkuk comes before the Lord with an honest but complaining heart, asking, "Why is there so much violence and evil and so little justice?"

You might be asking similar questions: "Why does the most immoral guy turn out to be the most popular guy? Why does the bully who harasses everyone always get his way? How can my Christian friends who once committed to stay sexually pure experiment with sexual gratification and sin? Why do bad things happen to good people?"

The Lord received Habakkuk's complaints graciously, just as He will receive yours. Through Habakkuk's experience, we have a model for intentional living.

infuse (in FYOOZ): to cause to be permeated with something (as a principle or quality) that alters usually for the better

> I will stand my watch and set myself on the rampart, and watch to see what He will say to me, and what I will answer when I am corrected. Then the LORD answered me and said: "Write the vision and make it plain on tablets, that he may run who reads it. For the vision is yet for an appointed time; but at the end it will speak, and it will not lie. Though it tarries, wait for it; because it will surely come, it will not tarry. Behold the proud, his soul is not upright in him; but the just shall live by his faith." **—Habakkuk 2:1–4**

Habakkuk intentionally made his way up the steps to the rampart, where only a few soldiers and little noise awaited him. He needed to hear a new voice, a heavenly voice. There, above the crowd and the noise of the city, he would not be distracted.

If we are serious about hearing from God in a personal way, to be led by His Spirit into intentional living, we have to get away from the noise and distractions of the locker room, the chat room, and the mall. We need to get away from human voices and into the quiet of our own private world.

In your quiet time with God, you can think clearly without the opinion of others or the noise of the culture. Through this time, focus on rebuilding your inner strength and making good choices.

Decide to reject man's opinions and value God's truth about:

+ your potential,

+ choosing friends,

+ making decisions,

+ defining morality, and

+ what is important in life.

Deal with unfinished emotional business, such as:

+ dreams you haven't started or finished and

+ relationship issues you need to work out.

Establish peaceful habits, such as:

+ planning and organizing your life,

+ studying, reading, and learning new skills,

+ spending time with interesting people, especially mentors, and

+ turning off the radio, iPod, Internet, and TV for at least one hour a day.

Genuine pearls are an expensive luxury. But years ago, a shortcut was developed. Scientists found that if a foreign object was injected into an oyster, it would cause an extreme irritation. In defense, a shiny, beautiful pearl quickly formed around the object. It looked perfect on the outside, but when X-rayed, the pearl was found to have a "false heart."

What time of day can you set aside one hour to sit without external noise and work on one of the peaceful habits above?

GROUP DISCUSSION

What is it that usually gets in the way of having quiet, alone time?

Habakkuk was ready for God to speak. *Are you ready?*

What can you do about it?

Intentional living is fueled through spiritual intimacy with God. The spiritual experience Habakkuk was seeking was not a church service or a Bible study with friends. He wanted to hear from God personally, and he wanted to improve the condition of his heart. He wanted a two-way conversation with God.

In your time with God this week, consider these questions: *What will God say? How will I respond? How will I change? What will I answer when I am corrected?*

Habakkuk admits that there is unfinished business in his heart. He knows that God will lovingly correct him, and he welcomes it. This kind of revolutionary heart change does not come about through casual prayer or glancing through Scripture. Our great God loves us intimately, and He longs to have a genuine, two-way relationship with us.

> When you reach for the stars, you may not quite get them, but you won't come up with a handful of mud either.
> —Leo Burnett

Intentional living fuels purpose in everyday life. It requires daily quiet time with God. Schedule it, and don't let anything or anyone rob you of that time. In your quiet time, initially switch your habits and do a few new things such as:

+ listening to music that exalts Christ,

+ reading through the Psalms, or

+ developing the habit of writing in a journal—positive thoughts, words of gratitude, your feelings.

This time may be quiet, but its results will rock your world as you are empowered and changed, strengthened and enthused to live every day with excellence. It can happen!

Do you dread time alone with God because you think of Him as angry, waiting to punish you and put you down? It's true that God hates sin, but He longs to forgive you and fill you with confidence through love. Correction does not equal anger. God's intentions are the best for you—always. Come to Him in your quiet time with anticipation of His forgiveness and care for you.

There are days when it seems like everyone in the world is talking, and no one is listening. On those days when your parents don't seem to listen and your friends don't seem to care, and even the dog won't come when called, you can be sure that the Creator of the universe is leaning His ear out of heaven in anticipation of hearing you speak.

He loves you so intensely that He gives you this promise: "Then you will call upon Me and go and pray to Me, and I will listen to you" (Jeremiah 29:12).

Write the verse again below and substitute your name for "you."

_____

_____

_____

diffuse (di FYOOZ)', to pour out and permit or cause to spread freely; to extend, scatter

> But without faith it is impossible to please Him, for he who comes to God must believe that He is, and that He is a rewarder of those who diligently seek Him.
> —Hebrews 11:6

The result of spiritual intimacy in your personal relationship with God is an intentional life that puts integrity, sincerity, and honesty on public display.

In the day of Habakkuk, it was common practice to publish anything of public concern. They did this by engraving tablets of smooth stones or wood in large letters and then hanging the engraving high on a public place to be read.

In Habakkuk 2:2, God commands Habakkuk to put His words on public display: "Write the vision and make it plain on tablets, that he may run who reads it." Habakkuk was to make God's words public in three ways:

+ *Make it plain*—so that everyone can see it.

+ *Write it clearly*—so that people can understand it.

+ *Write it enthusiastically*—so that those who read it will run to tell others.

What does your life, put on public display for others to read, say? Your reputation for intentional living should be talked about in the halls so that others will see it and enthusiastically join you in living for Christ. How can this happen? Living intentionally means that you carefully choose every thought, motive, and action. Your life is defined by integrity, sincerity, and honesty.

Integrity comes from the Latin word for wholeness. The Christian cannot divide his or her life into compartments: "This one is for God; this one is for me." You can't give God Sunday mornings or Wednesday nights and then take the other days as your own. Indeed, if Christ is Lord of your life, then He is ruler and master. He has the first word and the last word.

> We need people who influence their peers and who cannot be detoured from their convictions by people who do not have the courage to have convictions.
> —Joe Paterno, legendary Penn State football coach

Do you have compartments in your mind? Any specific thoughts you don't want to give up?

Sincerity keeps the promises you make to God and to yourself, regardless of whether or not there are consequences, such as:

+ Treating everyone kindly regardless of popularity.

✦ Following through on a peaceful habit.

Honesty causes you to make moral choices even if no one is looking, such as:

✦ Giving back change when the teller accidentally gives you too much.

✦ Telling the cashier that she forgot to charge you for the socks.

✦ Not giving in to temptation when you think no one is watching.

The intentional life also displays a willingness to trust God for His timing. Today, we rely on instant messaging, high-speed Internet, and fast food—but God is not on instant or fast mode. We can't name the date when God will answer our prayers. A person who lives intentionally chooses to wait on God for a life of distinction and influence.

Habakkuk went to the rampart because he wanted an answer—and God gave him one. He said, "Wait and see what I will do at the appointed time." Habakkuk came away from the wall with this conclusion: "The just shall live by his faith" (2:4).

What about you? Is there a root of bitterness, broken promises, unfaithfulness, or playing with sin in your life? If so, like Habakkuk, admit to God that you have unfinished business with Him, and wait expectantly for His loving correction.

To be rightly related to God, we must have faith in His Word and His timing. When you are not embarrassed to say that you choose to wait on God, then you have showed the world genuine faith. And as we have learned, daily, genuine faith is fueled by intentional living.

FUSE BOX

Intentional living causes me to carry out the commitments of my heart long after the emotion of a decision is gone.

When you face the defining moments of your life, you do not want to have a false heart because you did not wait on God to develop you emotionally, spiritually, and physically with purity.

PRIVATE WORLD DEVOTIONS

MONDAY: See it. Read the surrounding passages or chapter for the Key Scripture so that you can get an understanding of the background and context. This helps you to really *see* the verse.

TUESDAY: Hear it. Read the daily Key Scripture and/or surrounding passage out loud, putting your name in, if applicable. For example, John *can do all things through Christ. Thieves have come to destroy* John, *but Jesus has come that* John *might have eternal life.*

WEDNESDAY: Write it. Write the verse and then what it says about:

+ *Others:* Respond, serve, and love as Jesus would.
+ *Me:* Specific attitudes, choices, or habits.
+ *God:* His love, mercy, holiness, peace, joy, etc.

PRIVATE WORLD JOURNAL

I am grateful for—I praise you for—I am feeling—I am thinking—I need help with

PRIVATE WORLD DEVOTIONS *(Continued)*

THURSDAY: Memorize it. Take the verse with you—write it on a card or put it in your phone, iPod, or PDA. Go over it throughout the day so that it begins to *live* in your heart and mind.

FRIDAY: Pray it. Personalize the verse as you pray for yourself or for others or in praise to God. To pray is literally "to think about." Try thinking out loud or writing in your **PRIVATE WORLD JOURNAL**.

SATURDAY: Share it. Ask the Lord to bring someone to mind or in your path today who needs good news. Don't be shy—just let it out! Whether you IM, write, text, tell, or send it, the joy of God's Word will flow from your heart into theirs.

PRAYER REQUESTS

Date	Name	Need	Answer

PRIVATE WORLD JOURNAL

I am grateful for—I praise you for—I am feeling—I am thinking—I need help with

NOTES

CHAPTER 3

EXECUTION
THE ART OF GETTING THINGS DONE

KEY SCRIPTURE

Why should a living man complain, a man for the punishment of his sins? Let us search out and examine our ways, and turn back to the Lord.
—Lamentations 3:39–40

COULD THIS BE YOU?

Stephan Bekale was fifteen when he left his home in Tchibanga, Gabon, and stepped off the plane at JFK International Airport in New York. Although he didn't know anyone in America and only had seventy-five dollars in his pocket, he was one step closer to his dream of playing professional basketball. He practiced his basketball skills, spent a year raising money for the plane ticket, contacted the U.S. embassy to obtain a visa, and concentrated on his schoolwork so that he would be competitive not only as an athlete but also as a student.

With continued determination, Stephan positioned himself for a place on a high school team. He contacted a coach with an excellent program, and within a few weeks Stephan was living in Virginia and playing high school basketball. He kept his grades up, received a full scholarship to Penn State

> Obstacles don't have to stop you. If you run into a wall, don't turn around and give up. Figure out how to climb it, go through it, or work around it.
>
> —Michael Jordan, all-time greatest NBA player and a student cut from his high school team

his senior year, and kept his eye on the dream of playing in the NBA.

In his first semester at Penn State, Stephan received word from Africa that his father had died of AIDS. Soon after, the disease also claimed his mother's life. After that, Stephan recalls, "I was not as hungry as much as I was. I told myself maybe I should educate young kids. Young kids in Africa."[1]

His basketball dreams didn't seem as important, and instead he focused on raising money for water purification systems and other needs in Gabon.

"For I know the thoughts that I think toward you," says the LORD, "thoughts of peace and not of evil, to give you a future and a hope [an expected end]".
—Jeremiah 29:11

After graduating with a B.S. in business administration, Stephan passed on his dream of the NBA and focused on a new goal. He used his talents, knowledge, and skills to build Hoops 4 Africa, an organization that uses the influence of NBA and WNBA celebrities to raise awareness of the HIV/AIDS virus among African youth and delivers a message of safety and prevention of the virus. Through basketball clinics this fall in Kenya, Stephan and ten players from the NBA and WNBA will reach out to children, teens, and adults with a message of hope that could save their lives.[2]

WHY KNOW IT?

✦ 60 percent of adults wish they had spent more time on obtaining good grades in high school.[3]

✦ 69 percent of Americans believe that more needs to be done concerning poverty in our nation.[4]

✦ Only 48 percent of Americans volunteer their time for any type of charity.[5]

transfuse (trans FYOOZ) ; to cause to pass from one to another; transmit

Deep within all of us are nagging insecurities about our capacity for leadership: *How can I change the world when I can't even change me? How can I motivate others if I lack motivation myself? How can I lead others if I can't even lead myself?* The answer lies in a progressive strategy of examining our inner lives and executing necessary changes.

> *But be doers of the word, and not hearers*
> *only, deceiving yourselves. For if anyone*
> *is a hearer of the word and not a doer, he*
> *is like a man observing his natural face*
> *in a mirror; for he observes himself, goes*
> *away, and immediately forgets what kind*
> *of man he was.* **—James 1:22–24**

When you look in the mirror, who do you see and what changes need to be made?

infuse (in FYOOZ) ; to cause to be permeated with something (as a principle or quality) that alters usually for the better

There are four types of people described below. As you read about the four types, look for characteristics in each description that you identify with.

Wishers. These people try to wish things into being. They say things like, "I wish I had a new car." "I wish I was popular." "I wish I had more money or more education." These people need to stop wishing on the stars and start reaching for them.

Common traits of Wishers:

+ They talk about doing things but seldom get started on them. "Someday" is the most-used word in their vocabulary.

+ They discuss their possible plans, but they never set goals. Then they keep talking about why the plans won't work.

+ They are sideliners. On any given Friday night, they would rather watch *SportsCenter*'s Top 10 plays of the day than risk trying out for the team.

Complainers. These pessimists see only problems and not possibilities. They don't think of looking for a solution or accepting a challenge. It's easier to keep complaining than to try to make a difference.

Complainers have their own language, often using the following phrases:

+ It's not fair.

+ I never have good luck.

+ It won't work.

- ✦ It's not my fault.

- ✦ Nobody likes me.

- ✦ That's too much work.

- ✦ I don't have the _____ (time, money, friends, opportunity, etc.) to succeed.

Sleepwalkers. Sleepwalkers have no idea what is going on at any given time. They are usually late for everything, can't find what they need, and forget facts, people, and responsibilities.

When a Sleepwalker encounters a problem, his or her common responses are:

- ✦ Apathy: "I don't care."

- ✦ Visionless: "It's not my problem."

- ✦ Gutless: "Whatever makes you happy."

These first three types of people—Wishers, Complainers, and Sleepwalkers—can often be present in one person at the same time, because their common thread is meaningless double-talk. James called these people "double-minded," meaning a mind that changes like the wind changes direction. He goes on to say, "Let not that man suppose that he will receive anything from the Lord; he is a double-minded man, unstable in all his ways" (James 1:7–8). In sharp contrast to the double-minded person is the fourth type of person— the single-minded doer.

> Why should a living man complain, a man for the punishment of his sins? Let us search out and examine our ways, and turn back to the LORD.
> —Lamentations 3:39–40

Doers are set apart from all the rest. While everyone else complains, sleeps, and daydreams, the Doers are actually making plans and executing them.

Consider the traits of a DOER:

Depend on the power of God to provide.

Overcome obstacles, limitations, and habits.

Execute dreams.

Risk failure.

Now that you know about the four different types of people, ask yourself, "Which one am I? Which one would I like to be?"

What is ONE THING I can do to become the type of person I want to be?

Effective leaders subject themselves to periodic self-examination. *Examine,* from the Greek, is to "prove" or "test" your state of mind.

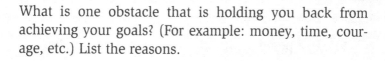

GROUP DISCUSSION

What is one obstacle that is holding you back from achieving your goals? (For example: money, time, courage, etc.) List the reasons.

How can you "climb it, go through it, or work around it"?

"Be doers of the Word, and not hearers only" (James 1:25). This Greek word picture speaks not just of physical action but of an active mind. It is also used as an imperative, making it a command of God.

The exciting life of a doer is contrasted with the person who is a *hearer* only. Maybe you have been one of those people—sitting in church, listening to the sermon, singing the songs, closing your eyes during the prayer, and maybe even putting in an offering, and then thinking, *Hey, I've done what I am supposed to, and now I'm done.*

diffuse (di FYOOZ): to pour out and permit or cause to spread freely; to extend, scatter

The Hebrew word *shamea*, translated "to hear," means both to hear and to obey, making it clear that one does not exist without the other. So then, a sermon is not truly *heard* unless it moves you to *do*.

 A **Doer** of God's Word:

✦ Has a positive attitude in the face of difficulty.

✦ Does not blame God or others when things go wrong.

✦ Is consistent in values and does not change with the circumstances.

✦ Has control of tongue and temper.

✦ Puts faith into practice and on display.

The "hearer only" doesn't follow through. Instead he "observes himself, goes away, and immediately forgets what kind of man he was" (James 1:24). He sees the dirt on the face, the messed-up hair, and thinks, *I need to wash my face and comb my hair.* But the moment he is away from the mirror, he forgets to do it. Complacency and mediocrity crowd out effort and excellence.

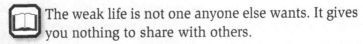 Obviously, in James 1:23–25, the mirror is the Word of God. In His love and care for us, God speaks, and we see the need to scrub clean areas of our heart. But when we get away from the Word, we forget and keep walking through life unchanged. We settle for the boring life of a wisher, complainer, and sleepwalker.

The weak life is not one anyone else wants. It gives you nothing to share with others.

[FUSE BOX]

The mirror of Christ shows us two views: *who we are* and *who we can be* for Christ.

Satisfaction lies in
the effort, not in
the attainment; full
effort is full victory.
—Gandhi

PRIVATE WORLD DEVOTIONS

MONDAY: See it. Read the surrounding passages or chapter for the Key Scripture so that you can get an understanding of the background and context. This helps you to really *see* the verse.

TUESDAY: Hear it. Read the daily Key Scripture and/or surrounding passage out loud, putting your name in, if applicable. For example, <u>John</u> *can do all things through Christ. Thieves have come to destroy* <u>John</u>, *but Jesus has come that* <u>John</u> *might have eternal life.*

WEDNESDAY: Write it. Write the verse and then what it says about:

+ *Others:* Respond, serve, and love as Jesus would.

+ *Me:* Specific attitudes, choices, or habits.

+ *God:* His love, mercy, holiness, peace, joy, etc.

PRIVATE WORLD JOURNAL

I am grateful for—I praise you for—I am feeling—I am thinking—I need help with

PRIVATE WORLD DEVOTIONS *(Continued)*

THURSDAY: Memorize it. Take the verse with you—write it on a card or put it in your phone, iPod, or PDA. Go over it throughout the day so that it begins to *live* in your heart and mind.

FRIDAY: Pray it. Personalize the verse as you pray for yourself or for others or in praise to God. To pray is literally "to think about." Try thinking out loud or writing in your **PRIVATE WORLD JOURNAL.**

SATURDAY: Share it. Ask the Lord to bring someone to mind or in your path today who needs good news. Don't be shy—just let it out! Whether you IM, write, text, tell, or send it, the joy of God's Word will flow from your heart into theirs.

PRAYER REQUESTS

Date	Name	Need	Answer

PRIVATE WORLD JOURNAL

I am grateful for—I praise you for—I am feeling—I am thinking—I need help with

NOTES

CHAPTER 4

VISION
A 360° VIEW

KEY SCRIPTURE

*If we confess our sins, He is faithful and just
to forgive us our sins and to cleanse
us from all unrighteousness.*

—I John 1:9

COULD THIS BE YOU?

After years of starring in movies with casual drug use and sex that bordered on porn, Stephen Baldwin wasn't an obvious candidate to become a Christian. However, when his wife, Kennya, hired a nanny named Augusta, something extraordinary happened. Augusta didn't focus on who her new employers were; instead, she focused on the vision of who they could become.

Before coming to work for the Baldwins, Augusta had prayed and felt God leading her to a family that would come to know Christ and start a ministry. She sang songs about Jesus while she worked in the Baldwin home, and one day Kennya asked her why she always sang about God. Augusta happily shared with her that she believed God was using her to lead the Baldwins to Him.[1] Kennya shared this idea with Stephen, and they laughed about it. But in the weeks that followed, Kennya asked Augusta more and more questions and even began studying the Bible with her.

> Vision is a clear picture of what *could* be, fueled by the conviction of what *should* be.
> —Andy Stanley

The Baldwin family eventually moved, and Augusta went to work for someone else. But in the three years she was with the family, she made an impact. Once they settled in New York, Kennya began attending church regularly and accepted Christ. The next year Stephen watched his wife grow spiritually, read the Bible, and pray for their family each day. "She never pushed it on me, never pointed a finger, never judged me. I was becoming extremely curious about what that experience was. Because she wasn't faking it, and it was a mighty powerful thing," recalls Stephen.[2] Soon, Stephen started reading the Bible, praying, and attending church with his wife. Shortly after the tragedy of September 11, 2001, Stephen committed his life to Christ and was baptized.

Christ has given Stephen peace and helped him to be a better father and husband, and he is not afraid to share his testimony with others. "In my position, I just don't think I'm supposed to keep my faith to myself," says Stephen.[3] His position as an actor has allowed Stephen to share his faith in national television interviews and as a motivational speaker at schools. The ministry Augusta believed Stephen and Kennya would have is still evolving through partnerships with CBN, skate park evangelism, and many youth-focused ministry events.

WHY KNOW IT?

+ 70 percent of those who read Focus on the Family's *Plugged In* magazine say they watch R-rated movies.[4]

+ 44 percent of adolescents say they watch something different when they're alone than with their parents. 25 percent choose MTV.[5]

+ 50 percent of Americans believe that anyone who is "generally good or does enough good things for others during their life will earn a place in heaven."[6]

transfuse (trans FYOOZ): to cause to pass from one
to another; transmit

How many times have you needed to borrow money, and a friend said, "If I had it, I'd give it to you"? Then you have other friends who have the money, but they don't volunteer to give it. Wouldn't it be great if you could combine those two people into someone who could help you? You can—God is that person. He has all power, and He wants to give it to you.

In the year that King Uzziah died, I saw the Lord sitting on a throne, high and lifted up, and the train of His robe filled the temple. Above it stood seraphim; each one had six wings: with two he covered his face, with two he covered his feet, and with two he flew. And one cried to another and said: "Holy, holy, holy is the Lord of hosts; The whole earth is full of His glory!" And the posts of the door were shaken by the voice of him who cried out, and the house was filled with smoke. —Isaiah 6:1–4

Isaiah the prophet came onto the scene with a threefold message from God:

1. The holy one of Israel is *willing* to help you.

2. The holy one of Israel is *able* to help you.

3. The holy one of Israel *will most certainly* help you.

Isaiah had walked into the temple to mourn. King Uzziah—greatly loved by the nation, a man who at one time lifted up honor to God—was gone. The king who had once brought in enemy accounts of other kingdoms being destroyed, laid them out in the temple, and stood to proclaim, "We will trust the Lord," was gone. He wasn't a perfect man, but Isaiah had confidence in him and could work with him. Now there were a new set of rulers—Uzziah's ungodly sons, who would most likely make life for Isaiah unpleasant, to say the least.

It was not a good time for a prophet, and Isaiah was depressed. If you had watched him walk into the temple, he probably would have had his hands in his pockets (if robes had pockets back then), his face looking down, his hair a mess, and a look of dread on his face. But while he was looking down at the circumstances, God spoke to his heart and said, "Hey, Isaiah. Look up here, dude."

infuse (in FYOOZ) : to cause to be permeated with something (as a principle or quality) that alters usually for the better

Sometimes after we've had a setback or discouragement, we are ready for a breakthrough and a fresh understanding. God knows that, and He is ready to step in. Here Isaiah was quickly reminded that there is another King who sits upon the throne, and He not only rules, but He *overrules*. He is large and in charge.

The throne of heaven is still occupied. There may be confusion and unrest on earth, but there is perfect peace in heaven. God is seated in power and glory. Don't be content to see from a human perspective; start to see from God's perspective.

Isaiah says, "I saw the Lord sitting on a throne, high and lifted up" (v. 1). He received an exalted view of God, the One who lives above the circumstances. Suddenly, he received a new, fresh vision of God, His holiness, and His majesty. He started to look at things from God's point of view. It had a profound impact on him, so much so that twenty-nine times in the book of Isaiah, he refers to God as "the holy one of Israel."

What happened next was amazing. This fresh understanding of God overpowered everything Isaiah was worried about as he shifted his focus to the majesty of God. His worry, fear, and discouragement began to appear insignificant and ridiculous when He saw the Lord.

GROUP DISCUSSION

Ours is the most spiritual generation in decades. No one is really wrong, the culture says, and tolerance demands that every view is to be respected. But truth cannot be absolute or potent if it is merely relative. This soft view of values is ludicrous when compared to the absolute holiness of God—don't you think?

Isaiah saw the Lord in His holiness and cried out, "Woe is me, for I am undone! Because I am a man of unclean lips, and I dwell in the midst of a people of unclean lips; for my eyes have seen the King, the Lord of hosts" (Isaiah 6:5). The natural progression from seeing the holiness of God is what I call "The Inward Look."

CONFLICT RESOLUTION:

People berate, belittle, get angry, and break the relationship.

God confronts, forgives, and strengthens the relationship.

The Inward Look causes us to see our sin. Isaiah's new view of God immediately changed his view of himself and others. Tolerance wasn't even on the radar. The God of the Bible confronts us with our own sin and tells us, "I love you just like you are, but I love you too much to leave you that way."

When tolerance in our own lives is erased, we seek forgiveness for sin, and God is faithful to forgive. As 1 John 1:9 tells us, "If we confess our sins, He is faithful and just to forgive us our sins and to cleanse us from all unrighteousness."

What is ONE THING you can write below to confess:

Pray: "Lord, help me to see the sin of _____ the way that you do."

God's attitude is that sin cost Him His only Son. He hates sin, so He isn't interested in simply hearing you blurt out a list of sinful behavior while you proclaim, "I'm guilty." He is concerned about your attitude toward that sin and what you intend to do about it. When we confess, we agree with God about our sin. How does He feel about sin? God hates sin as much as He loves the sinner.

It is only when we change our attitude about the sin that entraps us that we are able to let go of it and it of us. The grip is gone because we no longer have an attachment to it.

Let's look at it this way. If tomorrow you walk into the school cafeteria and see a sign that says, "Spinach, broccoli, cauliflower, and liver are prohibited from being served or eaten in this room," do you think you could handle that OK? Would you mind terribly much? Now if you see a sign that says, "No chocolate, candy, cookies, ice cream, cake, pizza, chips, or snacks of any type will be allowed in this room," it might be a little more difficult to keep the rule. Why? You probably enjoy one and don't care much about the other.

Sin is the same way. When you think about it, crave it, desire it, it's hard to walk away from sin. But, when you *confess it*—that is, think of it in the same way God does—then you learn to dislike and even hate sin so that you are more than willing to pass it up.

diffuse (di FYOOZ); to pour out and permit or cause to spread freely; to extend, scatter

The power of The Inward Look doesn't lie in our own power of self-control but in understanding who God is and aligning ourselves with His passion for holiness. Because God's love is so complete, it changes us first and then fills us with a capacity and yearning to care about others in a fresh way.

The Inward Look leads us to The Outward Look. We start to see others not as obstacles or objects, but as opportunities. We look for ways to pray for, to encourage, and to share with those around us because our motives are pure and our selfishness is banished. We don't gossip about, judge, or discuss others.

A true spiritual experience humbles you and awakens a renewal within you. Isaiah confessed his sins to God, saying, "Woe is me, for I am undone! Because I am a man of unclean lips" (v. 4). His next thought was, *Hey, these people have the same problem. I can help.*

Everything up until now was preparation. Isaiah is no longer wrapped up in himself, held back by worry, sin, or discouragement. He has *seen the Lord,* and he understands that God is in charge. Now he is ready to go to work.

I heard the voice of the Lord, saying: "Whom shall I send, and who will go for Us?" Then I said, "Here am I! Send me." —**Isaiah 6:8**

There were three entities in the room: Isaiah, the seraphim, and the Lord. Isaiah was a mere human, and an unclean one at that, by his own admission. The seraphim was a heavenly being—fiery, faithful, and fantastic. But when it came time to make a difference in the world, who got the job? It wasn't the seraphim; it was Isaiah—a flawed human being.

Today, God continues to ask, "Whom shall I send, and who will go for Us?"

This is the life you've been waiting for! It's more exciting than being a rock star, more daring than a Saturday night party on the beach, and far more thrilling than any sexual or chemical experiment. It's a life of purpose that has a lasting impact on your generation.

When Isaiah walked out of the temple that day, he left his mourning at the altar and became a man on a mission. No longer a spectator, he was now a participant.

[FUSE BOX]

Are you content to stay up late Saturday night, come to church tired Sunday morning, eat dough- nuts, listen to the music, sit through the Bible study, and leave the same way you came in?

Confess: to agree with or have the same attitude about.

PRIVATE WORLD DEVOTIONS

MONDAY: See it. Read the surrounding passages or chapter for the Key Scripture so that you can get an understanding of the background and context. This helps you to really *see* the verse.

TUESDAY: Hear it. Read the daily Key Scripture and/or surrounding passage out loud, putting your name in, if applicable. For example, <u>John</u> *can do all things through Christ. Thieves have come to destroy* <u>John</u>, *but Jesus has come that* <u>John</u> *might have eternal life.*

WEDNESDAY: Write it. Write the verse and then what it says about:

+ *Others:* Respond, serve, and love as Jesus would.
+ *Me:* Specific attitudes, choices, or habits.
+ *God:* His love, mercy, holiness, peace, joy, etc.

PRIVATE WORLD JOURNAL

*I am grateful for—I praise you for—I am
feeling—I am thinking—I need help with*

PRIVATE WORLD DEVOTIONS *(Continued)*

THURSDAY: Memorize it. Take the verse with you—write it on a card or put it in your phone, iPod, or PDA. Go over it throughout the day so that it begins to *live* in your heart and mind.

FRIDAY: Pray it. Personalize the verse as you pray for yourself or for others or in praise to God. To pray is literally "to think about." Try thinking out loud or writing in your **PRIVATE WORLD JOURNAL.**

SATURDAY: Share it. Ask the Lord to bring someone to mind or in your path today who needs good news. Don't be shy—just let it out! Whether you IM, write, text, tell, or send it, the joy of God's Word will flow from your heart into theirs.

PRAYER REQUESTS

Date	Name	Need	Answer

PRIVATE WORLD JOURNAL

I am grateful for—I praise you for—I am feeling—I am thinking—I need help with

NOTES

CHAPTER 5

OPTIMISM
A COUNTERCULTURAL MIND-SET

KEY SCRIPTURE

Only do not rebel against the Lord, nor fear the people of the land, for they are our bread; their protection has departed from them, and the Lord is with us. Do not fear them.

—Numbers 14:9

COULD THIS BE YOU?

All eyes were on the new guy. Rumors were everywhere, and the story was out: Matt was here as a last resort. After he had been kicked out of school and arrested for drugs, his mom shipped him off to live with his dad. Dad called the church for help, and the youth pastor invited Matt to come to the Wednesday night youth event.

> The bigger your God, the smaller your obstacles.

No one in the youth group talked to Matt because they didn't know what to say. He looked different—spiked hair streaked with fluorescent red, piercings in his nose and lip, and a definite attitude. Students ignored him, and the youth workers were afraid of bringing him into the group. Once the gossip started, it was hard to stop, and Matt could tell he wouldn't be fitting into this church crowd.

One young man, a college student volunteer, saw Matt across the room and began to pray for him. While everyone else gave a negative report, Lockwood thought, *I can win this guy to Christ. He isn't hopeless.* Lockwood walked over and invited Matt to step out of the room for a soda. Matt agreed, anxious to leave the stares behind. As Lockwood listened, Matt shared his heart about the emptiness and the lure of drugs to fill the void. After an hour of listening to Lockwood share the gospel, Matt bowed his head and received Christ as his Savior.

It happened because one young Christian believed the best about a guy whom everyone else believed the worst about. Lockwood gave a good report about Matt, and God honored it.

WHY KNOW IT?

✦ 24 percent of people age 16 to 24 volunteer their time.[1]

✦ Making a difference in people's lives ranks in the top ten goals teenagers have for their lives.[2]

✦ Teens at the top of their class are twice as likely to volunteer their time for charity or social service activities.[3]

transfuse (trans FYOOZ)*,* to cause to pass from one to another; transmit

The negative student looks at life and asks, "What can they do for me? Who can I blame? What can I get?" In contrast, the student leader looks at life and asks, "How do I join in? What can I give to make a difference in the world?"

Students who are highly productive and emotionally healthy do not blame others, complain about circumstances, or live in the past. Their first word is positive. Their first word is honest and true. Their first word is their best word.

*Then Moses sent them to spy out the land of
Canaan, and said to them, "Go up this way into
the South, and go up to the mountains, and see
what the land is like: whether the people who
dwell in it are strong or weak, few or many;
whether the land they dwell in is good or bad;
whether the cities they inhabit are like camps
or strongholds; whether the land is rich or poor;
and whether there are forests there or not. Be
of good courage. And bring some of the fruit
of the land." Now the time was the season of
the first ripe grapes.* **—Numbers 13:17–20**

Moses sent out twelve spies to go and see what the
Promised Land was like. For forty days, these twelve
men spied out the people and the land. All of them were
sent out with the same instructions, but they returned
with conflicting accounts. How could this happen?

Easy. Each man reported his opinion from his own
point of view, and most of it was negative. If they started
out negative, they came back negative. If they started out
positive, they came back positive.

*The people who dwell in the land are strong;
the cities are fortified and very large; we saw
the descendants of Anak [giants] there...And
they gave the children of Israel a bad report
of the land which they had spied out, saying,
"The land...devours its inhabitants, and
all the people whom we saw in it are men
of great stature...We were like grasshoppers
in our own sight, and so were we in their
sight."* **—Numbers 13:28, 32–33**

The negative guys couldn't come up with one good thing to say about their own people—only about the impressive size and strength of the enemy. They had an agenda: to give a bad report about the Promised Land and to get the rest of the crowd on their side.

infuse (in FYOOZ) : to cause to be permeated with something (as a principle or quality) that alters usually for the better

Negative Attitude Is Fueled by Negative Emotions

Fear: "We're scared. They're bigger and stronger. Let's not try it."

Selfishness: "This doesn't work for us. It's too hard, and we're not willing to make the sacrifice."

Insecurity: "We're too small. We're like grasshoppers, and they are giants."

Negative Emotions Lead to Negative Behavior

After the negative report was given, the people fell apart emotionally. They completely lost it! Take a look ...

> *So all the congregation lifted up their voices and cried, and the people wept that night. And all the children of Israel complained against Moses and Aaron, and the whole congregation said to them, "If only we had died in the land of Egypt! Or if only we had died in this wilderness! Why has the Lord brought us to this land to fall by the sword, that our wives and children should become victims? Would it not be better for us to return to Egypt?" So they said to one another, "Let us select a leader and return to Egypt." — Numbers 14:1–4*

- ✦ **Fear** took control of the Israelites' emotions, and they cried like babies.

- ✦ **Selfishness** took center stage and started to rule with complaining.

- ✦ **Insecurity** led them to imagine the worst, even to the point of complete exaggeration.

Finally, they quit, gave up, abandoned all hope, and went backward. They were willing to forget the miracles of God, the work they had done, the progress they made, and the pain they endured so far. The vision died, and its killer was faith in the negative report.

These ten men were chosen as leaders to represent their individual tribes, but they were leaders in name only. They were classic *grasshopper thinkers*: make lots of noise, be small in thought, and have no direction or goal but self.

diffuse (di FYOOZ) ; to pour out and permit or cause to spread freely; to extend, scatter

> *Then Caleb quieted the people before*
> *Moses, and said, "Let us go up at once*
> *and take possession, for we are well able*
> *to overcome it." —***Numbers 13:30**

> *Only do not rebel against the* LORD, *nor fear the*
> *people of the land, for they are our bread; their*
> *protection has departed from them, and the* LORD
> *is with us. Do not fear them. —***Numbers 14:9**

It was easy to be part of the negative crowd that day. You could blend right in, give a few grunts, and no one would bother you. But the positive guys had a different spirit. Two guys out of twelve, two guys out of a mob who accepted the negative report, two guys of a *different spirit* stepped forward and stepped into history.

Joshua and Caleb stood strong against the other ten spies. They urged the Israelites to keep believing, saying of the Amalekites, "They are our bread"—or as we might say, "We'll eat them for lunch!" Joshua and Caleb believed in a big God, One who keeps His promises, One who has the power to do whatever needs to be done.

Joshua and Caleb were courageous leaders, and their example of the good report is one for all of history to learn from. What set them apart from the rest of the crowd?

Focus: Joshua and Caleb were just as tired as everyone else, but they refused to take their eyes off the prize. Joshua kept the memory in his mind and heart of the day Moses told him, "God is giving us this land," and he held on to that promise as absolute truth.

+ **Focus on the promise already received.** Joshua received God's promise of this land as a young guy, probably a teen, and he held on to it as a focused goal throughout his life. He developed the habit of optimism as a young man, and the result was a positive report just when it was needed.

+ **Focus on the truth, not on the opinion of the crowd**. Joshua and Caleb refused to listen to negative gossip. They didn't reason or fret or pick apart the negative report. They just stepped up to the front and gave a positive, good report.

GROUP DISCUSSION

The habits below will enable you to focus on truths rather than opinions. Consider how the following would affect your daily conversations if you:

+ Don't listen to negative reports.

+ Depend on God's resources and abilities rather than your own.

+ Base your convictions on faith and truth.

+ Develop the habit of optimism first.

What is ONE THING negative that you have to deal with that you could turn around by focusing on the habit of thinking with optimism?

Faithful: Joshua spent his young life learning from the great leadership of Moses. This lifelong commitment to a faithful life prepared Joshua for the day when he would be called upon to give a good report and stand against the crowd.

Practice faithfulness on a daily basis.

> *So the Lord spoke to Moses face to face, as a man speaks to his friend. And he would return to the camp, but his servant Joshua the son of Nun, a young man, did not depart from the tabernacle.* **—Exodus 33:11**

✦ When Moses was alone before God at Sinai, Joshua kept watch.

✦ He learned character, patience, and meekness from Moses as well as valor and tenacity.

✦ He learned teamwork as Moses worked closely with Aaron and with Eleazar the priest. As a result, Joshua was able to work closely with Caleb.

✦ He learned that sometimes a leader serves and sometimes a leader leads, and both are necessary to get the job done.

Demonstrate courage in your leadership.

Only do not rebel against the LORD, nor fear the people of the land, for they are our bread; their protection has departed from them, and the LORD is with us. Do not fear them. —**Numbers 14:9**

✦ Believe in yourself and God's will for you.

✦ Point out the positive first in every situation.

✦ Proclaim courageous faith in the promises of God.

✦ Replace fear with faith.

How important was the mentoring of Moses in the life of Joshua?

What about in your life? Would you consider being disciplined enough to serve alongside a spiritual mentor? Begin praying for a spiritual mentor who can be an example to you as Moses was to Joshua.

📖 Finish strong.

Joshua was not about to give up on his dream of a Promised Land because of a few negative reports. He not only stepped up as an optimistic leader, but he went on to become a great leader of the nation of Israel. His last address to Israel confirms he finished the race with the same commitment and courage with which he began it: "Now therefore, fear the Lord, serve Him in sincerity and in truth, and put away the gods which your fathers served on the other side of the River and in Egypt. Serve the Lord!" (Joshua 24:14).

> The quickest way to be defeated is to be distracted.
> —General Norman Schwarzkopf

Caleb stood at the age of eighty-five and thundered, "Give me that mountain where the giants live!" Joshua and Caleb were finishers and became the only two men from that generation who were able to enter the Promised Land. The rest of that generation died in their complaints while the land waited for the Israelites to receive it.

How do we finish strong in our lives, like Joshua and Caleb did?

✦ Don't settle for the natural when you have the supernatural.

✦ Adjust your vision through the eyeglasses of faith.

✦ Declare a genuine, personal faith in God.

We all know people who step out loud and soon fade out. We've seen Christians who talk righteousness and judge others and yet fall out into sin themselves. This is truly discouraging, especially if they are close friends or people we look up to.

What does your reputation say about being faithful to the finish?

_____

_____

_____

Unbelief sees problems; faith sees solutions.

_____

Think about a situation where you started out strong but didn't finish well. What do you think happened along the way?

_____

_____

_____

What can you do to develop the habit of optimism all the way to the finish line?

_____

_____

_____

FUSE BOX

It's easy to be part of the negative crowd today. You blend right in, go with the control of the crowd, look like and act like everyone else in the culture. But you have a *different spirit*. You are ready to step into history!

Multiply the length of your vision times the width of your commitment times the height of your conviction. The result is the volume of your influence.

PRIVATE WORLD DEVOTIONS

MONDAY: See it. Read the surrounding passages or chapter for the Key Scripture so that you can get an understanding of the background and context. This helps you to really *see* the verse.

TUESDAY: Hear it. Read the daily Key Scripture and/or surrounding passage out loud, putting your name in, if applicable. For example, John *can do all things through Christ. Thieves have come to destroy* John*, but Jesus has come that* John *might have eternal life.*

WEDNESDAY: Write it. Write the verse and then what it says about:

   ◆ *Others:* Respond, serve, and love as Jesus would.

   ◆ *Me:* Specific attitudes, choices, or habits.

   ◆ *God:* His love, mercy, holiness, peace, joy, etc.

PRIVATE WORLD JOURNAL

I am grateful for—I praise you for—I am feeling—I am thinking—I need help with

PRIVATE WORLD DEVOTIONS *(Continued)*

THURSDAY: Memorize it. Take the verse with you—write it on a card or put it in your phone, iPod, or PDA. Go over it throughout the day so that it begins to *live* in your heart and mind.

FRIDAY: Pray it. Personalize the verse as you pray for yourself or for others or in praise to God. To pray is literally "to think about." Try thinking out loud or writing in your **PRIVATE WORLD JOURNAL.**

SATURDAY: Share it. Ask the Lord to bring someone to mind or in your path today who needs good news. Don't be shy—just let it out! Whether you IM, write, text, tell, or send it, the joy of God's Word will flow from your heart into theirs.

PRAYER REQUESTS

Date	Name	Need	Answer

PRIVATE WORLD JOURNAL

I am grateful for—I praise you for—I am feeling—I am thinking—I need help with

NOTES

CHAPTER 6

RESPONSIBILITY
THE ABILITY TO RESPOND

KEY SCRIPTURE

Jesus said to her, "I am the resurrection and the life. He who believes in Me, though he may die, he shall live. And whoever lives and believes in Me shall never die. Do you believe this?"
—**John 11:25–26**

COULD THIS BE YOU?

Jack was exhausted. He was working fifteen or more hours a day to get ready for a youth event, and his partner wasn't pulling her weight. The first time Tia didn't show up for the meeting, Jack let it slide. The second time he got angry, and he told everyone else about it but Tia. This time, he was trying to round up fifty students to start the class, and Tia wasn't there to help, again.

Jack lost it. He went to Tia and shouted at her, "Do you think you are so special that you don't have to work?" Next, he went to his youth minister and poured out his complaint. The youth minister listened to Jack's complaint and then asked, "Did you ever ask Tia about where she was?" Jack admitted he hadn't. That's when he got the real story.

Tia didn't show up for the meetings because she had been reassigned to work at the hospitality table. She wasn't supposed to be at the meeting. And, if he had taken the time to look around the room,

> Sometimes a person's reaction is not about what's happening in the moment, but rather a result of piles of emotion that haven't been dealt with.

he would have seen Tia in the corner counseling and praying with one student. That's why she wasn't rounding up the other forty-nine.

Jack overreacted because he was tired. His frustration caused him to react without getting information. If he had, he would have responded and encouraged his friendship with Tia instead of damaging it.

WHY KNOW IT?

✦ The prefrontal cortex acts as the CEO of the brain, controlling planning, working memory, organization, and modulating mood. This matures throughout adolescence until about age 25. As it does, teenagers learn to reason better, develop more control over impulses, and make judgments better.[1]

transfuse (trans FYOOZ)ʼ to cause to pass from one to another; transmit

What scientists can now prove by looking into the brain is what your parents have been trying to explain to you: You can't base your decision on your emotions at the time. That is why a wise student places himself under the authority of caring adults and surrounds him- or herself with godly friends. These work together to hold you accountable and to stand beside you in good choices as you become emotionally mature. Students benefit from the accountability and wisdom of others as their brains develop, especially in the area of controlling emotional impulses in order to make rational decisions.

This is not a cop-out or excuse for bad behavior, but it does explain some of the struggle within teens to make good, reasonable choices rather than emotional reactions as they navigate the bridge to adulthood.

Now it happened as they went that He entered a certain village; and a certain woman named Martha welcomed Him into her house. And she had a sister called Mary, who also sat at Jesus' feet and heard His word. But Martha was distracted with much serving, and she approached Him and said, "Lord, do You not care that my sister has left me to serve alone? Therefore tell her to help me." And Jesus answered and said to her, "Martha, Martha, you are worried and troubled about many things. But one thing is needed, and Mary has chosen that good part, which will not be taken away from her."—**Luke 10:38–42**

Tired Bodies = Reaction

Martha gave Jesus the classic "It's not fair!" speech. She was tired and stressed, but instead of recognizing the need to rest and prioritize her tasks, she *reacted* to Jesus and her sister, Mary.

Can you imagine the scene? Martha starts her pitiful, "Don't you care about what I'm going through?" tirade, followed by a "Make her help me" demand, while Jesus, the Son of God, is in her house, teaching about heaven. She had no idea of the history-making event in her living room because she was distracted from the wildly important. She allowed herself to get completely stressed over a second-best choice.

Jesus quickly *responded* with a teaching point—one that you and I must learn. He calmly responded to Martha that she was "worried and troubled about many things" (v. 41). He further explained that we must choose to focus on one task at a time, and it should be the "good part" or, literally in the Greek, the best choice. That best choice, Jesus went on to say, would "not be taken away from her" (v. 42).

Mary is remembered as the one who sat at Jesus's feet and ministered to Him, but Martha is known for her emotional outbursts.

infuse (in FYOOZ) : to cause to be permeated with something (as a principle or quality) that alters usually for the better

Before you make a decision, run it through the HALT principle—that is, never make a decision when you are:

Hungry

Angry

Lonely

Tired

 GROUP DISCUSSION

Have you ever made a decision or said something you regretted because you were

Hungry, **A**ngry, **L**onely, or **T**ired?

What is one decision you might respond to differently now that you know this principle?

You can start to make an immediate difference in your stress level if you make that change. Serve yourself an immediate cease and desist order!

 Leaders focus on the wildly important.

What is ONE THING you can choose to focus on this week?

_____

_____

_____

> *Then Martha said to Jesus, "Lord, if You had been here, my brother would not have died. But even now I know that whatever You ask of God, God will give You." Jesus said to her, "Your brother will rise again." Martha said to Him, "I know that he will rise again in the resurrection at the last day." Jesus said to her, "I am the resurrection and the life. He who believes in Me, though he may die, he shall live. And whoever lives and believes in Me shall never die. Do you believe this?" She said to Him, "Yes, Lord, I believe that You are the Christ, the Son of God, who is to come into the world."* **—John 11:21–27**

Lonely Hearts = Reaction

Once again, Martha lets her emotions rule her. This time, her brother's death so overwhelmed her that she blurted out to Jesus, "It's Your fault! If You had come when we asked you to, this wouldn't have happened." Martha *reacted* out of loneliness, and she needed to blame somebody, anybody, for her pain. It just happened that this time it was the patient, loving Christ, and He recognized a deeper need in her.

Jesus **responded** to Martha's emotional reaction with love. He saw that her irrational accusation was actually the symptom of a spiritual need. He asked her, "Do you believe?" Martha said the right words—"Yes, I believe"—but this was a powerless faith that could not fill her loneliness or give her genuine peace.

Sometimes someone with a weak personal faith can appear to be emotionally needy. When we strive to see people as Jesus sees them, we become more aware that they may need to be encouraged, to be comforted, or they may simply need someone to listen to them. Is there someone in your home or at school who sometimes reacts emotionally? Do you have that person in mind? Can you think of ways to respond to him or her with encouragement, comfort, or a listening ear? Ask God to help you do so this week.

"Lord, I pray for _____ and ask you to help me see him/her as you do this week. Help me to encourage, comfort, and listen."

diffuse (di FYOOZ); to pour out and permit or cause to spread freely; to extend, scatter

When I respond to a person's emotional reaction, I have the opportunity to show the love of Christ in action.

Anger and Hurt = Reaction

*Then He said: "A certain man had two sons. And the younger of them said to his father, 'Father, give me the portion of goods that falls to me.' So he divided to them his livelihood. And not many days after, the younger son gathered all together, journeyed to a far country, and there wasted his possessions with prodigal living. But when he had spent all, there arose a severe famine in that land, and he began to be in want. Then he went and joined himself to a citizen of that country, and he sent him into his fields to feed swine. And he would gladly have filled his stomach with the pods that the swine ate, and no one gave him anything. But when he came to himself, he said, 'How many of my father's hired servants have bread enough and to spare, and I perish with hunger! I will arise and go to my father, and will say to him, "Father, I have sinned against heaven and before you, and I am no longer worthy to be called your son. Make me like one of your hired servants."' And he arose and came to his father. But when he was still a great way off, his father saw him and had compassion, and ran and fell on his neck and kissed him." —***Luke 15:11–20***

We don't know what the emotional trigger was—maybe a sudden argument or months of unresolved conflict. In this case, the younger brother *reacted* in anger and said, "Give me my stuff—I'm out of here. My freedom and my fun are more important than anyone else's feelings or situation." He left home and family and went as far away as he could, spending money, living without rules. This angry reaction caused him to disrespect his father, forsake his family, and offend the treasured values of the day.

To demand and react is sin because we have within us the power to act peacefully and in love. The son couldn't see any of this because he was living in the fantasyland of a far country. At first, it was a blast; but just as suddenly as it began, it was over. He was broke and living with the pigs. Not exactly the good life. When he finally came to his senses, he realized his rebellion was sin, and he went home to seek his father's forgiveness.

This patient father **responded** with complete love and forgiveness. He focused on his love for the son and not on the sin his son had committed.

Think about it: If *reacting* is about me, then I need to be thoughtful about a conflict by focusing on improving the situation and not on anger at the person.

The leader looks beyond the conflict to the person and how he or she can be helped.

What ONE THING can you do differently so that you will not react in anger to your parents' discipline or questions?

Anger robs us
of a clear view of
life.

[FUSE BOX]

React: "It's all about me!"

Respond: "It's about the situation and how it can be improved or resolved."

Holding on to anger is like grasping a hot coal with the intent of throwing it at someone else; you are the one who gets burned.

PRIVATE WORLD DEVOTIONS

MONDAY: See it. Read the surrounding passages or chapter for the Key Scripture so that you can get an understanding of the background and context. This helps you to really *see* the verse.

TUESDAY: Hear it. Read the daily Key Scripture and/or surrounding passage out loud, putting your name in, if applicable. For example, <u>John</u> *can do all things through Christ. Thieves have come to destroy* <u>John</u>, *but Jesus has come that* <u>John</u> *might have eternal life.*

WEDNESDAY: Write it. Write the verse and then what it says about:

✦ *Others:* Respond, serve, and love as Jesus would.

✦ *Me:* Specific attitudes, choices, or habits.

✦ *God:* His love, mercy, holiness, peace, joy, etc.

PRIVATE WORLD JOURNAL

*I am grateful for—I praise you for—I am
feeling—I am thinking—I need help with*

PRIVATE WORLD DEVOTIONS *(Continued)*

THURSDAY: Memorize it. Take the verse with you—write it on a card or put it in your phone, iPod, or PDA. Go over it throughout the day so that it begins to *live* in your heart and mind.

FRIDAY: Pray it. Personalize the verse as you pray for yourself or for others or in praise to God. To pray is literally "to think about." Try thinking out loud or writing in your **PRIVATE WORLD JOURNAL.**

SATURDAY: Share it. Ask the Lord to bring someone to mind or in your path today who needs good news. Don't be shy—just let it out! Whether you IM, write, text, tell, or send it, the joy of God's Word will flow from your heart into theirs.

PRAYER REQUESTS

Date	Name	Need	Answer

PRIVATE WORLD JOURNAL

*I am grateful for—I praise you for—I am
feeling—I am thinking—I need help with*

NOTES

CHAPTER 7

CONSISTENCY
THE RIGHT TO INFLUENCE

KEY SCRIPTURE

And the peace of God, which surpasses all understanding, will guard your hearts and minds through Christ Jesus. Finally, brethren, whatever things are true, whatever things are noble, whatever things are just, whatever things are pure, whatever things are lovely, whatever things are of good report, if there is any virtue and if there is anything praiseworthy—meditate on these things.
—Philippians 4:7–8

COULD THIS BE YOU?

Jason felt the pressure. He knew if he didn't pass the math test, he wouldn't pass the tenth grade. When he complained to his friends, one of them came up with a solution: "Hey man, I know a brainy guy who will text message you the answers during the test. He charges five bucks for every answer." Jason had never cheated, but this seemed easy and foolproof.

Cheryl finally got Tim to ask her out. The problem was that it was for the same night that she had to write a paper for history. She was researching on line when a friend IM'd her, "Still need the paper? I

> And the God of peace will crush Satan under your feet shortly. The grace of our Lord Jesus Christ be with you. Amen.
> —Romans 16:20

found one for sale for $10 online." Cheryl thought, *If it's that easy, then everyone must do it.*

Marcus needed one more answer. He had to get a B on this test, but he had a mental block. He could see the girl beside him was already done, so he snapped a quick photo of her paper with his camera phone. He couldn't read it all, but he got just enough to get the answer right.

WHY KNOW IT?

+ 75 percent of high school students engage in serious cheating.[1]

+ 50 percent of high school students have plagiarized work they found on the Internet.[2]

+ 50 percent of high school students surveyed said they don't believe that copying questions and answers from a test is cheating.[3]

transfuse (trans FYOOZ): to cause to pass from one to another; transmit

If the focus is on impressing others, then shortcuts take over. The successful leader doesn't live for the moment, for events, or for everyone else's opinion.

Where do you live emotionally and spiritually on a daily basis, and who or what lives in you? If you want to be positive, you have to inhabit possibility—that is, God's available peace, power, and potential. When we do this,

When we understand that salvation is rooted in the divine and not the ordinary physical realm, then we start to grasp the available, genuine power of Christ, and we can face anything.

our lives exhibit *consistency*, and we earn the right to influence others.

> *And the peace of God, which surpasses all understanding, will guard your hearts and minds through Christ Jesus. Finally, brethren, whatever things are true, whatever things are noble, whatever things are just, whatever things are pure, whatever things are lovely, whatever things are of good report, if there is any virtue and if there is anything praiseworthy—meditate on these things.* **—Philippians 4:7–8**

Fear, worry, and anxiety have become a way of life for many people. One can hardly turn on the news, pick up a newspaper, or talk to a neighbor without hearing of crime, violence, disaster, and just bad news! How can our first word be positive if we are bombarded with junk on a daily basis?

Inhabit the Peace of God

> *And the peace of God, which surpasses all understanding, will guard your hearts and minds through Christ Jesus.* **—Philippians 4:7**

Not only can you banish fear, worry, and anxiety, but you can possess the gift of contentment. That is the peace of God—not having to run from one event to another or to look for people to hang out with in order to have fun, but being content and free to sit quietly as you plan, pray, and think. It is more than possible.

When you inhabit the peace of God, your heart is protected by a stronghold. Your life displays peace to others. We can't just sit in a room and ignore the pain of life. This powerful, stable peace of God will enable you to endure and give you the ability to overrule circumstance.

What circumstance are you facing that is robbing you of peace? (For example, a conflict at home, school, in a relationship, personal illness, learning problems, etc.)

Fill in your name in the space provided in the following verse, and read it aloud: "And the peace of God, which surpasses all understanding, will guard _____'s heart and mind through Christ Jesus" (Philippians 4:7 NKJV).

CONTRAST

The Greek religion of the day, Stoicism, taught people to be free of passion (suffering) through *apatheia*, the Greek word for apathy. They abolished all desires and eliminated emotion in order to find peace. The Stoic was to be self-sufficient.

Christianity teaches God-sufficiency and the peace of God, which results in great joy. Instead of the absence of emotion, Christ fills us with positive and strong emotions.

infuse (in FYOOZ)¦ to cause to be permeated with something (as a principle or quality) that alters usually for the better

Inhabit the Mind of Christ

Your next move is to *inhabit the mind of Christ* as your own.

We all admit that:

✦ we have seen pop-up ads on the Internet we never wanted to see, and

✦ we have been surprised at language and scenes on TV and in PG or PG-13 movies.

 GROUP DISCUSSION

Negative language and images permeate the culture. What can you do to maintain a consistent mind? It's not a job for wimps. The current of the culture is strong, and you have to be strong and fit to swim against it.

What does the mind of Christ think? Philippians 4:8 tells us how to inhabit the mind of Christ: "Finally, brethren, whatever things are true, whatever things are noble, whatever things are just, whatever things are pure, whatever things are lovely, whatever things are of good report, if there is any virtue and if there is anything praiseworthy—meditate on these things."

The key here is the word *meditate*, which is to dwell on, to think about continually. It is the beginning of a consistent mind.

Meditate on *whatever is* ...

✦ *True*—that which will not let you down or vary with opinion.

✦ *Noble*—that which has the dignity of holiness upon it.

✦ *Just and pure*—that which is morally undefiled, meaning it is fit to be brought into the presence of God and used in His service.

✦ *Lovely*—that which calls forth love, encouragement, health and well being.

✦ *Of good report*—it is positive and beneficial for man and God to hear.

✦ *If there be any virtue*—virtue is defined as *moral excellence.*

Moral excellence involves the very heart of who you are. Develop the habit of choosing to think the best about every situation. Anyone can see error and what is wrong, but few people look at a situation daily and see what is right or what can be done to make it better.

Inhabit What You Know to Be Truth

You already know that Christ died for you and that He rose from the dead to pay for your sins and to give you victory over them. Jesus said, "I am the way and the truth and the life" (John 14:6). So you know that He is absolute truth, that He offers abundant life, that He is all-powerful, and that you have not been left to your own power to be positive. As Romans 3:37 says, "Yet in all these things we are more than conquerors through Him who loved us."

A focus on absolute truth prevents you from being tossed about by despair or discouragement. You stay consistently positive and look for new possibilities in life. When you inhabit the possibilities of God, your first thought is consistently positive. People will listen to you, watch you, and be positively influenced by you.

diffuse (di FYOOZ) ; to pour out and permit or cause to spread freely; to extend, scatter

Inhabit the Possibilities of God

When we are overwhelmed with the sin of this planet, we must remember that God's mercy is deep enough to bear it so that there is hope for anyone to come to Him. Try to dwell on this: His is a love so great and His mercy so deep that He can and will receive and redeem anyone who comes to Him, regardless of his or her past.

Set your mind on things above, not on things on the earth.
—Colossians 3:2

This God of patience, of comfort, and of consolation speaks to us about a confident life. His is not the patience of "hanging on" or "I hope I'll make it." His is endurance with joy that gives the ability both to bear things and to rise up and conquer them.

Christ offers strength that is infused throughout the mind and heart, literally filling and overflowing through our being with potential for good.

He is not only the God of peace, but He is the God of grace, of hope, and of patience. "Now may the God of hope fill you with all joy and peace in believing, that you may abound in hope by the power of the Holy Spirit" (Romans 15:13).

An inhabited understanding of the grace of God keeps one from despair about self; an inhabited understanding of the overruling providence of God keeps one from despair of the world.

 When you inhabit the mind of Christ, your first response is to serve. Only when you think of the needs of others first do you have the right to influence them.

FUSE BOX

The influential leader is one whose life is CONSISTENT—consistently believable because of the words, attitude, and actions he or she presents daily.

I can do all things through Christ who strengthens me.
—Philippians 4:13

NOTES

> What lies behind us
> and what lies before
> us are tiny matters
> compared to what
> lies within us.
> —Ralph Waldo Emerson

PRIVATE WORLD DEVOTIONS

MONDAY: See it. Read the surrounding passages or chapter for the Key Scripture so that you can get an understanding of the background and context. This helps you to really *see* the verse.

TUESDAY: Hear it. Read the daily Key Scripture and/or surrounding passage out loud, putting your name in, if applicable. For example, John *can do all things through Christ. Thieves have come to destroy* John, *but Jesus has come that* John *might have eternal life.*

WEDNESDAY: Write it. Write the verse and then what it says about:

✦ *Others:* Respond, serve, and love as Jesus would.

✦ *Me:* Specific attitudes, choices, or habits.

✦ *God:* His love, mercy, holiness, peace, joy, etc.

PRIVATE WORLD JOURNAL

I am grateful for—I praise you for—I am feeling—I am thinking—I need help with

PRIVATE WORLD DEVOTIONS *(Continued)*

THURSDAY: Memorize it. Take the verse with you—write it on a card or put it in your phone, iPod, or PDA. Go over it throughout the day so that it begins to *live* in your heart and mind.

FRIDAY: Pray it. Personalize the verse as you pray for yourself or for others or in praise to God. To pray is literally "to think about." Try thinking out loud or writing in your **PRIVATE WORLD JOURNAL.**

SATURDAY: Share it. Ask the Lord to bring someone to mind or in your path today who needs good news. Don't be shy—just let it out! Whether you IM, write, text, tell, or send it, the joy of God's Word will flow from your heart into theirs.

PRAYER REQUESTS

Date	Name	Need	Answer

PRIVATE WORLD JOURNAL

I am grateful for—I praise you for—I am feeling—I am thinking—I need help with

NOTES

CHAPTER 8

TENACITY

UNSTOPPABLE FORCE

KEY SCRIPTURE

And the Lord *said to Moses, "Why do you cry to Me? Tell the children of Israel to go forward."*
—Exodus 14:15

COULD THIS BE YOU?

Growing up in Hawaii with surfer parents, it was natural for Bethany to take up the sport. At age four, she won her first competition, and her parents joked that she must have "saltwater in her veins."[1] She was a professional surfer at age eleven, and by thirteen she was well respected in the surfing community. But one day in October, while surfing off Kauai's North Shore, Bethany's dream was shaken when a fourteen-foot tiger shark attacked her.[2] She survived the attack in spite of losing 70 percent of her blood, but she lost her left arm.

> Fear is a terrible master, and the people of Israel were enslaved to it.

Most people didn't expect thirteen-year-old Bethany to get back in the water so quickly. She ventured out on her board just ten weeks later. It was a triumph for her just to get up and ride a wave into shore. No one expected her to compete again—no one, that is, except Bethany. By the end of the year, she'd secured a spot on the U.S. surfing team and has since placed in numerous competitions.[3]

Bethany's story threw her into a different kind of sea—one made up of reporters and admirers. But the spotlight doesn't just shine on her amazing ability to recover. Bethany has written a book, *Soul Surfer*, to share how her faith in God helped her through this experience and more. She shares, "One thing hasn't changed—and that's how I feel when I'm riding a wave. It's like, here I am. I'm still here. It's still me and my board—in God's ocean!"[4]

> Of all the liars in the world, the greatest may be your own fear.

Bethany encourages others by saying, "[People] can do whatever they want if they just set their heart to it, and just never give up, and just go out there and do it."[5]

WHY KNOW IT?

+ The average person faces 23 adversities a day.[6]

+ In 15 of 16 health studies, people with the more optimistic outlook had the better results when it came to recovery.[7]

+ Only 5 to 10 percent of people are able to sustain optimism into their adult years.[8]

+ People with a positive attitude—energetic, happy, and relaxed—are less likely to catch colds than people who are depressed, nervous, or angry.[9]

transfuse (trans FYOOZ)*,* to cause to pass from one to another; transmit

Standing on the threshold of independence, you might be tempted to go back to easier days or stand still for a while. The third choice is go forward in confidence. None of these choices are bad, but only one defines the rule of the leader, and that is to go forward with tenacity.

*When Pharaoh drew near, the children of Israel
lifted their eyes, and behold, the Egyptians
marched after them. So they were very afraid,
and the children of Israel cried out to the LORD.
Then they said to Moses, "Because there were
no graves in Egypt, have you taken us away
to die in the wilderness? Why have you so
dealt with us, to bring us up out of Egypt? Is
this not the word that we told you in Egypt,
saying, 'Let us alone that we may serve the
Egyptians?' For it would have been better for
us to serve the Egyptians than that we should
die in the wilderness." And Moses said to the
people, "Do not be afraid. Stand still, and
see the salvation of the LORD, which He will
accomplish for you today. For the Egyptians
whom you see today, you shall see again no
more forever. The Lord will fight for you, and
you shall hold your peace." And the LORD said to
Moses, "Why do you cry to Me? Tell the children
of Israel to go forward."* **—Exodus 14:10–14**

The people of Israel started out with a "high hand" (Exodus 14:8 KJV)—in other words, they must have been high-fiving each other left and right. What an amazing miracle! They went from tortured, beaten, impoverished slaves to free men and women on their way to the Promised Land. No wonder they were pumped.

Life was one amazing praise fest. Look what Jehovah did! As long as the Israelites looked ahead, life was great. But then a few began to look back, and when they did, they saw the pow-

Fear turns truth and courage into lies and cowardice.

erful Egyptian army. Now trapped between the enemy and the mammoth Red Sea, fear took over.

Look how quickly everything changed. They weren't under attack, but they were already talking about dying in the wilderness. They wanted to quit.

> When we are out of sync with God, we take it out on people, and relationships start to fail.

When Fear Enters the Heart, Negative Words Come Out of the Mouth

And when Pharaoh drew near, the children of Israel lifted their eyes, and behold, the Egyptians marched after them. So they were very afraid, and the children of Israel cried out to the Lord (v. 10). The Israelites started complaining as they "cried out to the Lord." They forgot all that He had done for them in the past and the promise He made about their future. All they could see was the fear of the present circumstance.

Fear Fixes Blame and Runs from Responsibility

Then they said to Moses, "Because there were no graves in Egypt, have you taken us away to die in the wilderness?" (v. 11). After the Israelites turned against God, they turned on Moses. Think about it—they begged to be set free, agreed with the plan, worked hard to get ready to go, and set about with their own free will, full of joy and excitement about the future. But fear reduced all that was good to one moment of blame: "Why have you so dealt with us, to bring us up out of Egypt?" (v. 11). All of sudden, they had no part in this, and it was all Moses' fault.

Fear Brings About Anger, and Anger Twists Every Conversation It Enters

Notice how they started criticizing Moses and trying to prove him wrong and unfit as a leader. They attacked him in an emotional fit by asking, "Why would you do something so stupid like this?

Fear Exaggerates the Severity of a Situation

Because there were no graves, have you taken us away to die? (v. 11). The Israelites decided that the only result of this situation could be death—and nothing in-between.

infuse (in FYOOZ)**,** to cause to be permeated with something (as a principle or quality) that alters usually for the better

 When you feel like quitting...

Don't! Endure, persevere, and stay strong. Make the decision, once and for all, to continue ahead. As long as any doubt remains, determination cannot overcome. As the Lord told Moses, "Tell the children of Israel to go forward" (v. 14).

Examine your progress. The children of Israel made it out of bondage! They were halfway to the Promised Land. It was just as far to go back to Egypt as it was to go across the Red Sea. You may be right at the finish line. Don't give up!

Plan new goals. Yes, right now. This is the time to plan what you will do *after* you achieve the first goal. See the finish line, and start to plan on what happens next. Our God is a God of planning. For example, He gave His plan to Moses in Exodus 14:15: "But lift up your rod, and stretch out your hand over the sea and divide it. And the children of Israel shall go on dry ground through the midst of the sea."

You might be staring so hard at the closed door that you miss the breeze blowing right through the open window beside you.

Be grateful. Moses should have immediately started recounting the miracles of God and where He brought them from. That alone would have given them the strength to sprint across the sea. What has God already done for you?

Turn weakness into strength. The weakness of the Israelites was fear, an absence of faith. Identify what is holding you back. Do you need to go around the weakness or eliminate it by growing stronger in that area?

> He who has begun a good work in you will complete it until the day of Jesus Christ.
> —Philippians 1:6

Redirect your thinking. Never let yesterday take up too much of today. The Israelites started reciting a modified past in order to justify going back. Moses tried to redirect their thinking by standing still, but God directed them to think forward thoughts.

Seek godly counsel. There was no other leader who could advise Moses, so God stepped in Himself. He's like that! No matter what else you do, find a godly friend to cry, laugh, think, and pray with. This alone will give you great clarity and strength.

diffuse (di FYOOZ): to pour out and permit or cause to spread freely; to extend, scatter

Fear erodes leadership and provides excuses to quit. When the Israelites cried out to Moses, "Let's go back," he made what at first appears to be a valiant statement: "Do not be afraid. Stand still, and see the salvation of the Lord, which He will accomplish for you today" (Exodus 14:13). It sounds good, doesn't it? Except it was wrong. God's plan was for the people of Israel to move forward, not to stand still.

GROUP DISCUSSION

Is there a situation in your life that you are thinking of quitting (school, relationship, job, serving on a team, etc.)? Do you want to:

_____ go back   or   _____ stand still?

Using the lesson above, what is the ONE THING you can do to change this situation and continue to go forward?

_____

_____

_____

The Lord came back to Moses with a question: "Why do you cry to Me? Tell the children of Israel to go forward." We have been called to strengthen and help others to stay on the track with tenacity. In a culture where students choose to give up on life, we must show the power of Christ that is available to every individual through genuine, personal faith in Christ.

Do you know someone who is close to or thinking about giving up? Perhaps they are discouraged, hurt, or fearful. What can you do to move him or her forward with tenacity toward the finish line? List below two ways we can do this.

✦ _____

✦ _____

God never intends for His leader to settle for second best, especially when He has already promised to do a great work. The Lord wasn't about to let Moses slide on this one. He had promised the land, and He expected Moses to take Him up on that promise. In fact, when you picture this scene, Moses must have looked pretty embarrassed when the Lord said, "Why are you complaining? Do what I already told you to do."

Fear is a complete absence of faith in our great God. What are some steps you can take to banish fear and build your faith?

FUSE BOX

The winner's circle is a great place to be, but you only get there by crossing the finish line. When you're tired, embarrassed, discouraged, and ready to quit, there's just one thing to do—keep going.

NOTES

Be a second-miler.
It's never crowded
because the majority
gets off at the
first-mile exit.
—Zig Ziglar

PRIVATE WORLD DEVOTIONS

MONDAY: See it. Read the surrounding passages or chapter for the Key Scripture so that you can get an understanding of the background and context. This helps you to really *see* the verse.

TUESDAY: Hear it. Read the daily Key Scripture and/or surrounding passage out loud, putting your name in, if applicable. For example, <u>John</u> *can do all things through Christ. Thieves have come to destroy* <u>John</u>, *but Jesus has come that* <u>John</u> *might have eternal life.*

WEDNESDAY: Write it. Write the verse and then what it says about:

✦ *Others:* Respond, serve, and love as Jesus would.

✦ *Me:* Specific attitudes, choices, or habits.

✦ *God:* His love, mercy, holiness, peace, joy, etc.

PRIVATE WORLD JOURNAL

*I am grateful for—I praise you for—I am
feeling—I am thinking—I need help with*

PRIVATE WORLD DEVOTIONS *(Continued)*

THURSDAY: Memorize it. Take the verse with you—write it on a card or put it in your phone, iPod, or PDA. Go over it throughout the day so that it begins to *live* in your heart and mind.

FRIDAY: Pray it. Personalize the verse as you pray for yourself or for others or in praise to God. To pray is literally "to think about." Try thinking out loud or writing in your **PRIVATE WORLD JOURNAL**.

SATURDAY: Share it. Ask the Lord to bring someone to mind or in your path today who needs good news. Don't be shy—just let it out! Whether you IM, write, text, tell, or send it, the joy of God's Word will flow from your heart into theirs.

PRAYER REQUESTS

Date	Name	Need	Answer

PRIVATE WORLD JOURNAL

I am grateful for—I praise you for—I am feeling—I am thinking—I need help with

Notes

CHAPTER 1—LEADER: THE TOTAL PACKAGE

1. Albert L. Winseman, "Does Leader Tenure Make a Difference in U.S. Congregations?" The Gallup Organization (3 May 2005). http://www.gallup.com/poll/content/?ci = 16117&pg = 1 (accessed 14 July 2005).

2. Ibid.

CHAPTER 2—FUELED: LIVE WITH INTENTION

1. Julie Ray, "U.S. Teens Walk Away from Anger," The Gallup Organization (12 April 2005). http://www.gallup.com/poll/content/default.aspx?ci = 15811 (accessed 14 July 2005).

2. Ibid.

3. "Sickness Can Be Price of Unbridled Stress," Aetna InteliHealth (18 April 2002). http://www.intelihealth.com/IH/ihtIH/WSIHW000/8271/8014/348809.html (accessed 14 July 2005).

CHAPTER 3—EXECUTION: THE ART OF GETTING THINGS DONE

1. "About Us: Founder," Hoops 4 Africa. http://www.hoops4africa.org/founder.htm (accessed 12 July 2005).

2. Darlene Superville, "Ex-College Hoopster Joins AIDS Fight," *Boston Globe* (17 June 2005). http://www.boston.com/news/nation/articles/2005/06/17/ex_college_hoopster_helping_africans/ (accessed 12 July 2005).

3. Heather Kiefer, "High School: Worst of Times or Best of Times?" The Gallup Organization (14 June 2005). http://gallup.com/content/default.aspx?ci = 14611 (accessed 13 July 2005).

4. Frank Newport, "Update: Americans' Satisfaction with Aspects of Life in the U.S." (17 January 2005). http://poll.gallup.com/content/default.aspx?CI = 14611 (accessed 13 July 2005).

5. Raksha Arora, and Lydia Saad, "Social Issues Activate Affluent Women," The Gallup Organization (5 April 2005). http://www.

gallup.com/poll/content/?ci = 15517&pg = 1   (accessed   13   July 2005).

CHAPTER 4—VISION: A 360° VIEW

1. "Religion and Ethics Interview: Stephen Baldwin." PBS (7 May 2004). http://www.pbs.org/wnet/religionandethics/week736/interview1.html (accessed 13 July 2005).

2. Ibid.

3. Marshall Allen, "Multi(per)plexed," *Christianity Today* (1 March 2004). http://www.christianitytoday.com/ct/2004/003/9.64.html (accessed 13 July 2005).

4. "Facts/TV Statistics," Parents Television Council. http://www.parentstv.org/ptc/facts/mediafacts.asp (accessed 13 July 2005).

5. *Americans Draw Theological Beliefs from Diverse Points of View,* The Barna Organization (8 October 2002). http://www.barna.org/FlexPage.aspx?Page = BarnaUpdate&BarnaUpdateID = 122 (accessed 13 July 2005).

6. Ibid.

CHAPTER 5—OPTIMISM: A COUNTERCULTURAL MIND-SET

1. Cassie Moore, "Tips for Getting the Most from High School and College Students Who Volunteer," *The Chronicle of Philanthropy* (2 June 2004). http://philanthropy.com/jobs/2004/06/10/20040610-285129.htm (accessed 13 July 2005).

2. George H. Gallup Jr., "Teens Aim for the Simple Things in Life," The Gallup Organization (6 January 2004). http://www.gallup.com/poll/content/?ci = 10282&pg = 1 (accessed 14 July 2005).

3. Charles McComb, "Teens and Social Service: Who Volunteers?" The Gallup Organization (27 May 2003). http://www.gallup.com/poll/content/?ci = 8500&pg = 1 (accessed 14 July 2005).

CHAPTER 6—RESPONSIBILITY: THE ABILITY TO RESPOND

1. Sara Spinks, "Adolescent Brains are Works in Progress," PBS *Frontline* (31 January 2002). http://www.pbs.org/wgbh/pages/

frontline/shows/teenbrain/work/adolescent.html (accessed 12 July 2005).

CHAPTER 7—CONSISTENCY: THE RIGHT TO INFLUENCE

1. Alexander Rafael and Emily Anderson, "College Life 2.0," *Current* (Winter 2004). http://msnbc.msn.com/id/6596310/site/newsweek (accessed 13 July 2005).

2. Kathy Slobogin, "Survey: Many Students Say Cheating Is OK," CNN (5 April 2002). http://archives.cnn.com/2002/fyi/teachers. ednews/04/05/highschool.cheating/ (accessed 13 July 2005).

3. Ibid.

CHAPTER 8—TENACITY: UNSTOPPABLE FORCE

1. "Bethany Hamilton," Wikipedia. http://en.wikipedia.org/wiki/ Bethany_Hamilton (accessed 13 July 2005).

2. "Bio," Bethany Hamilton. http://www.bethanyhamilton.com/bio. htm (accessed 13 July 2005).

3. "Then and Now: Bethany Hamilton," CNN (22 June 2005) http:// www.cnn.com/2005/US/05/09/cnn25.tan.hamilton/ (accessed 13 July 2005).

4. "Bio," Bethany Hamilton.

5. "Then and Now: Bethany Hamilton," CNN.

6. Paul Stoltz, "Creating Sustainable Optimism," Executive Forum (27 April 2000). http://www.executiveforum.net/pdfs/stoltz.pdf# search = 'quitters%20campers%20stoltz' (accessed 13 July 2005).

7. L. A. McKeown, "The Power of Positive Thinking," Web MD Health (27 July 2001). http://my.webmd.com/content/article/33/1728_ 84995.htm (accessed 13 July 2005).

8. Paul Stoltz, "Creating Sustainable Optimism."

9. Cherie Berkley, "Positive Attitude Fights The Common Cold," Web MD Health (22 July 2003). http://my.webmd.com/content/ article/71/81297.htm (accessed 13 July 2005).

ABOUT THE AUTHOR

Jay Strack, president and founder of Student Leadership University, is an inspiring and effective communicator, author, and minister. Acclaimed by leaders in the business world, religious affiliations, and education realms as a dynamic speaker, Jay has spoken to an estimated 15 million people in his 30 years of ministry. His versatile style has been presented across the country and in 22 countries, before government officials, corporate groups, numerous professional sports teams in the NFL, NBA, and MLB, to over 9,500 school assemblies, and at some 100 universities. Zig Ziglar calls Jay Strack "entertaining, but powerful, inspiring and informative."

NOTES

NOTES

NOTES

NOTES

NOTES

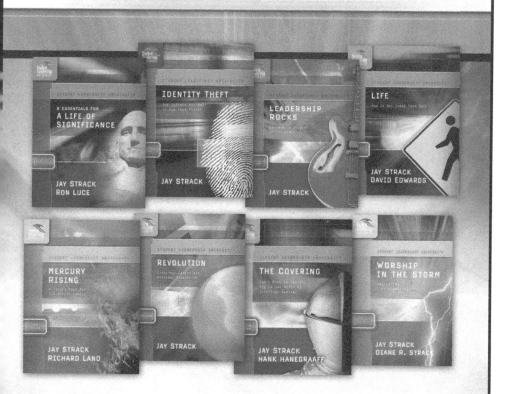